KNOW YOUR WEAPONS No. 3

ANTI-TANK WEAPONS

KNOW YOUR WEAPONS No. 3

ANTI-TANK WEAPONS

by

DEREK WHIPP

Fully illustrated throughout

The Naval & Military Press Ltd

Published by

The Naval & Military Press Ltd

Unit 5 Riverside, Brambleside
Bellbrook Industrial Estate
Uckfield, East Sussex
TN22 1QQ England

Tel: +44 (0)1825 749494

www.naval-military-press.com
www.nmarchive.com

ANTI-TANK WEAPONS.

SMASH THE AXIS TANKS.

Axis tanks must be smashed.

How?

Well, there are plenty of ways, but the Censor is naturally reluctant to let me tell you all the devices which the British Army employs. Nazis also read.

Nevertheless, within the confines of censorship, there are scores of things civilians should know something about. The regular army has special courses for tank-fighters, and other soldiers are taught things about meeting this form of menace. Because we can't all be in the Army, these pages are written with the intention of making people who are not recognised combatants useful guerillas rather than helpless evacuees. And if men in uniform pick up some knowledge, so much the better.

Much as everyone hopes his country will be saved from the horrors of tank invasion, such as many parts of Europe and the rest of the world have known, that possibility is by no means the product of wild imagination.

Spaniards succeeded in delaying tanks for two years—in spite of their almost negligible equipment. Russian guerillas also make the Nazi tank-driver's job one of the least pleasant in present-day conditions. After these examples, let it not be proved that the lessons they died to deliver have been wasted.

Before learning to use some of the weapons which will help to bust tanks, it would be as well to know how the Germans usually attack. Don't regard this as stereotype, though. The German High Command has a reputation for resource and cunning, and if one method proves too costly, you can be sure it has others ready to put into operation. Their tanks have not been built for ornament. And although throughout these pages reference is made principally to Germans, the lessons can be applied with equal success against Japanese and others—including even Italians

NAZI ATTACK.

THE Nazis have abandoned the 1914-18 principle of setting up lines of heavily-defended troops when it comes to attacking a similarly equipped group of defenders. They concentrate on breaking through the opposing forces at the weakest spot with mechanised units who push far ahead, leaving flanks open, and these advance units try to upset communications, try to cause panic and try to encircle bunches of defenders. They have succeeded sometimes.

Rather than advancing as a line, a Panzer column seeks to get through at one point, or perhaps a few points. Comparing an attacking force with a stick, instead of the two ends moving up parallel with the centre, the stick is turned round, and one end—sharpened or strengthened with tanks—is rammed in hard. The point attacked has shown itself in reconnaissance to be weaker than neighbouring areas.

Another analogy is the river embankment, with the Panzers represented by the water. At flood tide, the weak spot in the embankment is found; the water wears at this spot until a breach is caused; the trickle becomes a gush; the gush overpowers pieces of the much stronger defences near the hole; ultimately the dry land behind that embankment becomes flooded—with Nazis—and in that area even the firmest sections are left isolated.

The people eventually responsible for the embankment—the High Command—are unable to say whether it will hold, because those immediately concerned with local sections, in the form of divisional, battalion, or company commanders, are cut off by water from the places they would like to inspect and if necessary reinforce. The local commanders are unable to collect information.

However, the flood tide cannot maintain its volume for ever, and that accounts for the frequent stories heard during this war of troops who had been cut off finding their way back, undirected, through the enemy lines to headquarters.

This method of attack by which the Nazis flood their opponents is called deep infiltration in military parlance. Deep infiltration is by no means the copyright of the Nazis, but with the advent of mechanised forces, they succeeded temporarily in gaining the initiative by employing these tactics.

The counter to deep infiltration is defence in depth, and the Home Guard makes an ideal force for such a system. With compact bodies of men spread all over the country, infiltration cannot be pressed home as rapidly. Indeed, with men trained in field tactics and anti-tank methods, the price of advancing at all is very heavy.

Speed, up to now, has been the attacker's friend, because defending troops have not reached the invaded territory in time to engage the advance elements.

That same factor—speed—is all-important in overpowering a tank invasion. Descriptions of defence principles, however, will come later.

Let's imagine a tank advance is taking place somewhere. The Nazis have decided on the spot they will attack.

First of all come scouts on motor-cycles. They may spray civilians with machine-guns to create panic. There may be dive-bombers ahead of the scouts causing a lot more noise. Then, the rumbling of tanks is heard, and in fine weather dust clouds give the location. Usually, they approach in small batches, supported by anti-tank guns, by infantrymen in lorries, possibly by aircraft, and definitely by rumour. An impression of their method of advance can be seen in the illustration in the centre of the book.

THE FIRST LESSON.

So, if you read no further than this, you should know one way of minimising the power of a tank attack. *You must not exaggerate.* That is the first lesson. If you do, you will be helping the invader. It is very difficult to avoid exaggerating; the number of tanks, motor-cyclists, lorries or troops always seems far in excess of their true strength.

The same thing has occurred with air-borne troops, even

Infantrymen Deploying.

among regular soldiers. In Crete, for example, the total of reported parachutists and glider-troops was invariably over-estimated by trained troops who were perfectly well aware of the importance of giving accurate information. But it happened just the same.

If the column meets opposition, a halt is made and the supporting infantry may deploy in an endeavour to encircle. Meanwhile, the leading tank will perhaps fire a round or two, hoping to draw fire, and dive-bombers are probably brought up to try and blast a path if there is indication of opposition in strength—a feature of the German Army is that there is close co-operation between air and ground forces.

In spite of dive-bombers, though, the tanks can be held. It has been proved repeatedly during this war that dive-bombing does not do much killing. The thing it does most successfully is to create panic; and evidently from the type of bombs our enemy used in the early stages, he places fear high in the list of his offensive measures. From this, the moral is to concentrate on the ground and leave the aerial bombardment to those who cannot help being distracted.

Tanks are used as a sort of land cruiser fleet, ranging their guns against the defences. Mobile guns are cheaper than a number of emplacements, and they can be moved if a barrage becomes too accurate. On the other hand, the German dispatches were complaining in the winter of 1941 that Russians were fortifying their stationary tanks and using them as land batteries against the dug-in Nazis. It seems as though Russian tacticians were again one ahead of their foe.

The following particulars applied to Nazi tanks built before this war developed from its early stalemate condition and may not cover all the features contained in modern models. In fact, as this is being written, Press references to Nazis' armoured fighting vehicles carrying six-pounder guns are numerous. It will be seen that this weapon—the 75-mm. gun—originally featured only in the heavy-medium type.

Here is a rough classification of the armament on enemy machines:

(i) The short light model has two machine-guns;

(ii) The long type light carries an anti-tank gun and a machine-gun;

(iii) The light medium has a 37-mm. gun and a machine-gun;

(iv) The heavy medium is equipped with one 75-mm. gun and a heavy machine-gun, both of which fire from the main turret. A second machine-gun is in the fore turret, while another machine-gun is mounted on the third turret on the port side.

A further characteristic of some types is a flame-throwing device. This addition may occasionally be noticed because of a trailer attached with coupling bar and flexible hose. The trailer contains the inflammable fluid; and if the crew are so considerate as to reveal themselves they will be seen to be wearing asbestos clothing.

The driver of some models is equipped with a machine-gun firing independently of the turret. The weapon is fixed so that he can fire from the view obtained from his slit or periscope.

Tank-busters need to identify tanks as being friendly or enemy immediately they come into view. Further on you will read a warning about the possibility of Germans driving British tanks against our defences. The enemy has already captured some of our vehicles, and it would be inexcusable if defenders were lulled into inactivity simply because they could recognise a tank as British.

Such a contingency is to be guarded against by recognition signals given by the local command. Just as aeroplanes flying over this country are given unmolested passage when they prove themselves to be flown by Allied crews, so will tanks proceed unhindered only when they have established that they are not fighting "agin us."

For preliminary purposes it is necessary for defenders to know the characteristics of all tanks, and identification should reach the pitch which the Royal Observer Corps personnel have attained with aircraft. Tank-busters should become as enthusiastic in recognition as schoolboys were at one time in their ability to identify and name the makes of cars which passed them.

There are two certain ways of determining whether a machine is of Allied or Axis origin. At least, these charac-

Four Types of German Tank.

teristics obtain up to the time that this is being written, but tank design is by no means a static matter, because modifications and variations occur constantly.

The first difference is in the location of the wireless mast. On the British model, this is always attached to a point on the turret; the Germans fix theirs on the hull.

Difference number two is that the bogey wheels in the German models are usually evenly spaced and are of an even size. With our tanks, the wheels are uneven in space or size; sometimes uneven in both respects. An exception to this is the infantry tank, one of our "heavies."

One-Man Tank.

THE ONE-MAN TANK.

WHEN the Japanese first entered the war, much was made of their one-man tanks. As early as October, 1926, the Military Correspondent of the *Morning Post* forecast "No More Fighting On Foot," and described the one-man tank designed by Major G. le Q. Martel and driven by the designer on demonstration at Salisbury Plain.

In 1941, Major Martel became Major General Martel, Commander-in-Chief, Royal Armoured Corps.

As a matter of interest, a summary of the *Morning Post* report is included here.

"Originated and invented by Major Martel, the tank crossed a trench four feet wide, travelled at 15 to 20 miles an hour, weighed 2½ tons, measured 9 ft. by 4 ft., and stood 5 ft. high. The driver adjusted his seat with a lever which enabled him to sink below the protective armour. Otherwise, he drove from a position which gave him full view of the battle zone."

Like the Japanese model, it was equipped with a single machine-gun.

Yet another type of tank is the one capable of crossing stretches of water. These amphibians are necessarily armoured more lightly and therefore their vulnerability is increased. Both Russians and Germans have tried them out in actual combat, but their employment on a large scale has not caught the attention of military commentators or those who prepare communiques.

It can be said that the main tank used by the Germans is the "cruiser" type, carrying a crew of five men. There is one 75-mm. gun and two, or perhaps three, machine-guns. Its speed is about 25-30 miles an hour, and, as in most German models, is most vulnerable from the rear; that is to say, the defensive strength has been concentrated at the front.

The most notable constituent of a Panzer division is a tank brigade of two tank regiments, each of two battalions of 100 tanks. There is in addition a motorised infantry brigade, a mechanised artillery regiment, and other components, not the least of which is the repair unit.

In Norway, the Germans used light tanks in arrow-head formation. The infantrymen, protected by their vehicles, moved up immediately behind, and, according to a British soldier who was in Norway fighting against them, the co-operation between the mounted troops and those on foot was perfect.

An official description of the fighting on one sector in France showed that the Nazis used their aerial superiority to watch the progress of one tank battle. Eventually, the British were driven by 100 dive-bombers attacking for 20 minutes to abandon their anti-tank locations and a battle in open country ensued. Because of German numerical superiority in aircraft, tanks and troops, the British had to withdraw.

One fact emerging from these operations was that even at that stage, the British tanks proved equal to those used by

Infantrymen Protected by Tanks.

the Nazis at that time. The armour easily resisted direct hits by German anti-tank guns. The British 2-pounder anti-tank guns, on the other hand, penetrated all types of enemy tank, and the tracer often set them on fire.

The main conclusion was that until the British could claim to have equal numbers of tanks, they could neither expect to resist the German advance nor engage in a successful counter-attack.

WHERE TO STRIKE.

ALL this may give the impression—in print—that stopping tanks is an outsize job. It's certainly a fair size. Nevertheless, in spite of their thick skins, German armoured fighting vehicles are by no means irresistible.

Read on and learn a few things.

The most effective method of dealing with a tank is to range another against it. And if the enemy has ten thousand, then you must outnumber him—and yours must be protected more strongly and have greater fire power. Devastating tank battles have already occurred in Russia and Cyrenaica, with armoured units slamming at each other mercilessly. Germans in Libya, it has already been asserted, converted their cruiser tanks into mobile guns by stripping the armour and other accessories, leaving scarcely more than the "75" mounted on tracks. This seemed to indicate an urgent extemporisation, but events have shown that the Nazis believe it worth while to economise in protection for the attainment of greater speed and they have used this development extensively.

However, that side of tank-busting is beyond the scope of this booklet. The aim here is to discuss ways of destroying the effectiveness of tanks which roam unchallenged. Think of Spain for a second or two. . . . Recall how the Nazi and Italian vehicles were held for two years.

Achilles had but one vulnerable spot. No doubt, designers of these modern war horses would wish that their products had only one "heel." So far, they have not managed it.

It may seem paradoxical to say that the men inside are the weakest points in the machine. They are the main targets, and their lives should be made so uncomfortable that while advancing—in fact, at all times—their morale is at a low ebb. Every yard they proceed may bring them within reach of a new danger, and the fatigue produced by unrelieved tension, both physical and mental, can exhaust them to an extent that will produce a staleness which may

Weak Spots.

drive them into more vulnerable harbours than they would choose were they advancing through a country offering little opposition.

The alertness of the crews must be maintained to the point where human endurance rebels, and you may be one of those detailed to create that impossible condition for them. This wearing down process is dealt with elsewhere in the book, and we will see now the actual vulnerability in the machine itself.

The track is one of the weakest spots. Remove a tank from its track or smash a few links and the vehicle is immobilised until it can be repaired.

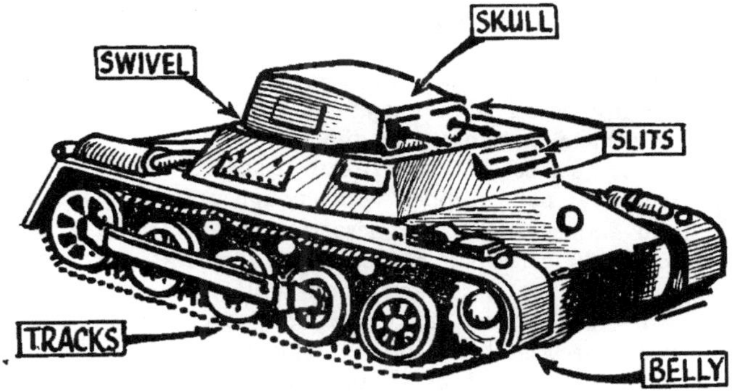

More Weak Spots.

In Spain, petrol-soaked blankets thrust into the track by unyielding Government supporters often succeeded. This had the effect of melting or burning the rubber cogs which engaged the tracks. Sometimes the blankets wound themselves round the driving wheel, or occasionally they ran along with the track and, still burning, started a fire in the fuelling system.

The Germans have learnt lessons, too, and the cogs are now made of less inflammable material. Therefore, it's not much good trying to emulate the Spaniards in this trick.

Nevertheless, since the Spanish war, the use of flames against tanks has developed, and more will be said later of this form of defence.

Rough or stony ground will increase the wear of the tracks and reduce the vehicle's mobile life. Divert them, if possible on to such surfaces, either by previously emplaced concrete blocks or mines, or by fire power.

ANTI-TANK RIFLE.

An anti-tank rifle plays havoc with the tracks of even the heaviest tanks. It fires .55 armour-piercing bullets and weighs about 37 lbs. Imagining the tank to be an ordinary car, the relative point of aim is immediately below the front mudguard. The anti-tank rifle makes a fearsome flash when fired and the report is considerably louder than the average small-arms.

The anti-tank gun is a quick-firing two-pounder of high penetrating power with a crew of five, who travel on the motor vehicle that tows the gun.

It is no secret that the British Expeditionary Force in Flanders was not equipped with enough anti-tank weapons, and an indication of the desperate measures adopted in France in the early part of this war is that anti-aircraft guns were brought to a flat elevation and used against Nazi A.F.Vs. Artillerymen, too, were firing over open sights.

Plenty has been heard of anti-tank mines, particularly in connection with the Libyan operations. The mines used by the British Army are capable of divorcing any tank from its tracks. They may be buried individually or strung together and drawn into the path of oncoming tanks. A pressure of as much as 300 lbs. is needed to set them off when they are prepared for detonation by tanks.

The tactics adopted by Republican fighters of the Spanish conflict have to some extent educated war departments throughout the rest of the world. The finest memorial, if ever a device for killing can be so described, to these Spaniards is the knowledge that the experiments they gave their lives to conduct provided the groundwork on which many modern anti-tank devices are based.

The dynamiters who went into battle with a lighted cigar between their lips, to be used for setting off the dynamite sticks they carried beneath their arms, share honours with the petrol blanket manipulators, grenade draggers and crow-bar wielders, all of them meaning with deadly earnestness to put into effect their slogan, "No passaran."

GETTING TO GRIPS.

THEIR process of ramming lengths of iron such as pieces of tram track or crowbars or even wooden spars between the tracks and the driving sprockets can be used to-day with effect. They waited behind cover, then, as the enemy approached, dashed out and crashed their battering rams into the weak spots.

Attacking the Track and Delivering a "Sticky."
(These operations are not performed simultaneously.)

You might think these people were particularly audacious in attacking literally within arm's length. But often that is the most effective way. Provided cover is available, a tank is most vulnerable when the tank-buster can get to grips with his prey.

The guns are useless inside fifteen feet because their traverse is limited, and the turret revolves slowly enough for an agile attacker—they should all be that—to hop out of the line of fire. There are complications, however. Flame-throwing apparatus might overpower the attacker. When the crew become desperate, they may use the slits from which to fire small arms.

One thing which is most likely to interfere with his operations is the protecting fire from supporting vehicles. Something else. Those infantrymen in the rear will take a chance or two when they see their cover being destroyed. They are not likely to remain inactive all the time.

The point between the turret and the body—the swivel—is vulnerable. A well-aimed shot will prevent the turret from revolving, and fire-power is restricted to one direction in those models where armament is concentrated within the turret.

When possible, a tank travels with the lid open, giving the crew plenty of ventilation and the commander maximum range of vision. The commander, travelling with his head above the turret, must be made to take cover inside his charge; a few rounds of small-arms fire will make him bob back.

The crew's discomfort will be intensified because of the reduced ventilation, and the field of vision is now limited to the periscope and slits provided for this purpose.

WEAK SIGHT.

Again, no hard and fast principles can be laid down, because some types have quite a few periscopes.

Numerous slits usually protected with bullet-proof glass, are placed around the machine. The most important one is that arranged for the driver, and others are provided for the convenience of the commander and gunners. If the bullet-proof glass is shattered, the slit will be useless for observation until the glass is replaced. Spares are carried for this purpose.

An alternative means of protection is to reduce the width of the slit to the minimum; this also further restricts ventilation and vision.

As soon as the defenders have persuaded the commander by means of small arms fire that hanging out of the turret is an unhealthy habit, his tank develops bad sight. Not necessarily shortness of sight, but the eye-sockets become sticky, as it were, and the eyes have difficulty in focusing objects outside the direct line of vision.

The crew have as much difficulty as a horse wearing blinkers of seeing anything but what is in front of their slits. And a horse has advantages which they lack. He can see what's going on at ground level as well as above him, but upward vision is poor in a tank because of the peaks protecting the slits.

So, the jack-in-the-box commander must be kept inside his flap, and the slits must be made to close to a minimum. We know that the less the crew can see the more vulnerable their fortress becomes.

The value of short-range attack is now obvious. And if protective or distracting covering fire is provided, determined troops can literally get to grips.

The crew should be harried by fire directed at the slits. It will be a difficult shot, particularly when the target is

Slit Trench Protecting Grenade Thrower from Blast.

moving, but if fire is held until the tank is so close that the marksman can aim upwards, the slit will present a good target. There is every reason to believe members of a tank crew when they say that to be in a tank when a round of .303 is ricochetting round the inside of a turret is not a pleasant experience. The periscopes also should receive the attention of marksmen.

The commander will do all he can to keep his vehicle moving, and riflemen will have difficulty in picking off periscopes and slits while the machine is travelling, but as soon as someone succeeds in busting the track or putting the driver out of action, or when the enemy sees an object which makes him halt, then the time is ripe for the riflemen to get busy.

Another way to render periscopes ineffective is for athletic men shod in light rubber footwear to jump on to the vehicles from cover and place tins or jars over these peep-holes. Sounds impracticable, perhaps, but it has already been proved effective.

Attack from ground level can be made by grenades. A slit trench or indentation which allows the grenade thrower to lie below the level of surrounding ground provides sufficient protection from blast and flying fragments.

THE THERMOS BOMB.

A THERMOS BOMB is one of the grenades to be used against A.F.Vs. It was designed specifically for use against them, in fact. Shaped something like a thermos flask, the filling consists of powerful high explosive.

Good cover is absolutely essential when using these things, because of the terrific blast. The grenade should be rested along the arm with the safety tape held in position by one finger.

The thermos bomb explodes on contact by means of a percussion fuse; therefore if it is to be dropped on soft ground it should be thrown high to give it enough force on impact to make the fuse work.

As with other grenades, a bowling action, either overarm or underarm, is the best method of delivery.

A safety pin holds up action of the fuse. Attached to this pin is a length of tape which remains in position by the safety cap.

The safety cap is removed before throwing, and as the grenade travels towards the target, the tape unwinds with the twisting of the missile. The percussion fuse now operates on impact.

Two spots where these grenades can do plenty of harm are the track and the suspension.

Heights such as the top of a bank or an upstairs window of a building have advantages for attacking tanks. An incendiary bomb, a Molotov cocktail or a sticky bomb dropped from such a position will seldom be noticed by the crew until it is doing its work. But remember those infantrymen at the back of the formation. They'll resent it if they're forced out into the open. Of course, there should be opposing infantrymen to look after them, but their first urge will be to get you.

The skull of the tank is often protected more lightly than the body. Another point to aim at is the belly.

FIRE, THE SERVANT.

ANTI-TANK ditches are too wide for a tank to negotiate in normal circumstances, but with bombers doing their best to blast a way through the defences, together with ground ordnance cutting up neatly arranged surface protection, vehicles will stand a greater chance of climbing across the spoiled sections of these ditches. When they can be caught with their bellies exposed, armour-piercing bullets will give them pains much more gruelling than acute appendicitis

And, while talking of stationary defensive devices, leaving an area undefended because a series of mines may hold up the tanks is just a development of the Maginot line mentality. Minefields must be guarded and efforts made by gunners, smoke screens and booby traps to divert tanks on to mined areas. There's another reason. Mistakes can occur, and it would be a tragedy if friendly tanks were lost because there was nobody about to warn them.

Flames and smoke, developing from the crude methods employed by the Spaniards, have now become a serious menace to the modern A.F.V.

Incidentally, the term A.F.V. incorporates auxiliary weapons-carriers, armoured infantry carriers, field guns and supply units. The tank is only one of many *A*rmoured *F*ighting *V*ehicles. Some of these accessory A.F.Vs. are open and may be discouraged from venturing too near the zone of operations by the more modern anti-tank weapons.

But the topic was flames and smoke.

AN

LT

Attacking a Soft Spot.

One of the most cumbersome of incendiary weapons was the petrol blanket. This contained a jam-jar or some other pot filled with petrol which seeped on to the material, and the contraption was ignited immediately before clapping into the track.

Following this, the Molotov cocktail made its appearance.

" Cocktail " is a blasé description for this weapon. It was improvised out of any sort of bottle strong enough to bear normal packing and transport, yet fragile enough to break easily on impact.

Experience provided a few lessons about these bombs. One was that quart beer bottles were both too heavy to throw any useful distance, and the glass was so tough that it did not always break. Similarly, pint beer bottles could not be relied upon to smash every time.

During an emergency, Molotov cocktails may still come in useful, so here is a description of their preparation.

Whisky, port or sherry bottles are the best to use, and their fragility can be improved by scoring downwards (from neck to base) with a diamond or other glass-cutting instrument. Scoring round the width of the bottle is likely to cause accidents; the bottle will possibly smash before it is thrown.

The contents? A mixture of equal proportions of petrol and tar make a nice, inflammable, sticky compound—though the fluid scarcely suggests the most palatable of cocktails, unless the hors d'œuvre has a generous basis of devilled tank. Gas oil, together with paraffin or naphtha is another combination which still lights easily and does not burn out straight away, at the same time being sticky enough to get a firm hold on the object at which it is directed.

Now a fuse.

In Spain they used matches which were not likely to be blown out in the wind, and these were attached to the bottles, one to each side of the neck, by adhesive tape. Celluloid strips, such as lengths of cinema film, will serve the purpose.

Such a fuse should be wrapped round the neck and kept in position by sticky tape, remembering to leave one end free for lighting. Alternatively, you can use cotton waste or rag tied to the bottle and dipped in an inflammable liquid and lighted before being thrown. But these things are not exactly toys, and messing about with such a fuse when it is wrapped round a bottle containing petrol or some such liquid is not to be encouraged unless the need is really urgent.

Something else: don't wrap the cotton waste round the centre of the bottle; if you do that, it is likely to act as a cushion when the bottle is thrown, and the glass won't break.

THE SELF-IGNITING PHOSPHORUS BOMB.

The necessity for lighting the fuse of the Molotov has always been a drawback, and the self-igniting phosphorus (S.I.P.) bomb was designed to overcome this difficulty.

The container is a bottle of comparatively fragile glass and resembles those used for mineral waters.

These, too, are nasty things to play with, for if one is dropped and the bottle broken, there appear fumes and flames apparently out of all proportion to the contents and lasting quite a few minutes.

It's not much good trying to put out the flames. Water or chemical extinguishers will kill them for a time, but when these have dried, a slight disturbance of the ground will cause them to burst out again. Better wait and let them burn out.

Phosphorus burns are worse than burns received by other means, because the liquid sticks to the flesh. Special treatment is necessary in the event of an accident caused through handling a S.I.P., and a summary is given here in case such an accident occurs.

Wash the burn with dilute alkali solution, such as ordinary washing soda, so as to neutralise the phosphoric acid.

With a solution of 1 per cent. of copper sulphate, wash for a second time. This creates a dark-coloured copper phosphide which has to be removed by tweezers or forceps.

For a third washing use an antiseptic solution such as boric acid or phenodine.

Where possible apply ultra-violet rays after the affected part has been dried. This treatment should last for a minute and a half from a distance of about two feet. The application of ultra-violet light should be given particularly in the case of severe burns. Strips of lint saturated in picric acid solution should then be applied daily for three or four days, then apply boric ointment dressings regularly. Phosphorus burns suppurate more than ordinary burns.

Washing the burn with sodium carbonate solution neutralises what phosphoric acid forms as a result of the combustion of the phosphorus, and the application of weak copper sulphate clears out the phosphorus remaining after the first washing.

Does the description of treatment just given impress you with the importance of keeping away from the fire these grenades produce? That is the intention; and you can appreciate now how it feels to be driving a tank when one of these has been broken on it.

Behind each tank there is usually a ventilation inlet, called a louvre. If it is possible to explode the S.I.P. grenade anywhere near this intake, the crew will suffer from the fumes and smoke as well as the danger to their tank from the flames. Perhaps it will be necessary to open the lid. In any case, a direct hit with one of these fire-raisers is generally enough to make the driver halt. He can't see where he's going. His warhorse is alight, and his pals want to breathe. If he goes on, he may run into an immobilising trap. So caution makes him halt.

A stationary tank is a much better target for our anti-tank weapons than one which is on the move. Anti-tank riflemen and gunners have more time and a better chance of securing a vulnerable hit.

Of course, when these marksmen open fire, the immobilised tank will reply with what fire power it can employ, but the advantage is with the defending forces if the S.I.P. has been well directed, for the tank gunners are firing through a cloud of fumes and smoke, whereas the stationary forces behind their various weapons and having the benefit of well-chosen cover, are directed to their target by the smoke. They wait until their sights are aligned on a particularly vulnerable spot, and let rip.

The most likely thing to happen when a S.I.P. registers on an A.F.V. is that the vehicle affected will be by-passed by the others in the unit who hope to create sufficient distraction for their lame member to receive treatment.

Another use to which these S.I.P. grenades can be put is for creating a smoke barrage. And, digressing for a moment, smoke is one of the most valuable aids when troops need to move during daytime. The enemy will fire at the smoke, but he's wasting ammunition unless he manages to put some of his opponents out of action. He can't keep a cone of fire directed at a smoke screen all the time it is hanging about. The defenders don't walk through the smoke but seek to envelop the enemy in the screen.

THE NORTHOVER PROJECTOR.

One way in which Britain took advantage of the delay in invasion was to produce a weapon capable of firing grenades.

The name of this piece of ordnance is the Northover Projector, after its designer. It is part of the equipment of all Home Guard units.

The Northover is capable of throwing the grenades several hundred yards maximum, though the most effective range is less. Mills bombs can also be projected. Care in loading these latter missiles is an almost unnecessary injunction.

The Northover is cheap to produce and simple to operate, with few defects or breakages likely to arise.

Various improvements have been introduced, and the latest model is a weapon worthy of the respect of the most offensive Panzer troops. Naturally, details cannot be disclosed.

The uses to which this weapon can be put extend beyond the immediate destruction or wounding of tanks. Valuable smoke screens may be laid, and it has potentialities against road blocks, enemy-occupied houses, barricades, and for the defence of beaches and aerodromes.

Some Home Guard units have exercised their ingenuity by producing armoured cars, and these have been used in manœuvres, much to the chagrin of their opposition. (The advantage of the surprise element has already been stressed.)

With good cover, it might be possible to move up the Northover mounted on such a vehicle. Generally speaking, though, the weapon requires a well-concealed site, for the barrel is a fair length and the trigger bar extends well beyond the breech.

Should your position as a Northover gunner become indefensible and the prospects of your weapon and ammunition falling into enemy hands become absolutely unavoidable, it is your duty to destroy them. The Nazi is always pleased when provided with weapons by his opponent, and you must forestall this possibility.

"Provided with weapons by his opponent." That phrase typifies a Nazi method. Do you remember how he found friends among the people whose country he invaded? Do you recall the way Czechoslovakian weapons were turned against that country with whom he appeared so anxious to make a peaceful settlement?

Remember the British h.e. and incendiary bombs dropped on Britain? And the Austrian Alpine troops used on Norway—from the Austria he declared he would not overrun—until he decided that the annexation of Austria was expedient?

These are Nazi methods. Friends for ever. But for them, the word "ever" means "until we can get more by making these friends our enemies."

Even British tanks may be used against us who have decided that the Nazis shall never find a resting place in Britain larger than a merited grave—and probably a com munal one, at that.

Therefore, until the defeat of a tank invasion is organised so well that regulars, Home Guards, guerillas, and all who would perish before they allowed their territory to become defiled by terrorist occupation can be confident that the tank they have found is a friendly one, that tank must be covered, or at least kept located, until word comes from a trustworthy source that there is proof that it is one of ours, driven by a friendly crew.

A worthwhile motto for all who find themselves in charge of an anti-tank weapon might be "In sight always, out of sights seldom." The object in those sights is, of course, the enemy vehicle.

Ambush with Sheet.

WORRY 'EM.

TANK drivers are quite prepared to carry on driving so long as they can see where they are going. Their training gives them the ability to assess the things which are visible as being worth while engaging or evading.

You know, however, that with the lid closed, their vision is restricted. So they cannot see S.I.P. bottles hung overhead—concealed in the lower branches of trees or camouflaged and pendant from telegraph crossbars. Occupying these points, they can be exploded by rifle fire, while the tank-busters take advantage of the smoke barrage and consolidate for an attack from all sides.

Sheet Ambush. Tank now Blinded.

The enemy knows the value of smoke, too. Part of their ammunition is made up of smoke shells. So there's not always smoke without enemy fire.

Armoured fighting vehicles have been stopped by the simple expedient of stringing one or two blankets round the bend of a road. The driver sails along until he comes to this point, where his vision is impeded. If he charges straight ahead, he may run through trip wires which set off all sorts of explosives; or he may crash straight into a sunken trap or other booby.

A development of the use of the blanket is for a sheet to be camouflaged to resemble the ground in a narrow lane. On either side of the lane is a man, and when the vehicle, travelling perhaps even quite slowly, is about to pass them, they each drag on a piece of rope or wire running through the edge of the sheet and passing over tree branches or gateposts. The sheet rises from the ground, and before the tank can stop it is completely enveloped and blinded.

Of course, sites have to be chosen discriminately, but if the scheme is well conceived and executed, there is no more effective way of rendering the crew sightless. It now falls to the attackers to dig the invaders from their shell.

Such a simple device as arranging a string of soup plates across the ground will make the driver hesitate. What's under those things? What are they? Those are the questions he will ask himself. They may conceal nothing. They may, on the other hand, conceal newly planted tank mines. He has to stop and observe—he may even spend a few rounds of machine-gun ammunition—before he feels confident enough to advance. Meanwhile, the grenade throwers or gunners are preparing a suitable reception.

RUSSIAN TACTICS.

A book describing the tactics employed by guerillas operating near Pskov in August, 1941 gives a good account of one way in which Nazi tanks were trapped.

The authoress tells how German sentries directed night traffic along a certain road by lights, stopping the drivers from taking a branch road leading into marshland. Before the occupation, the road was used by carts to take reeds to a nearby factory.

In the marsh was an island—the camp for another guerilla force. The two bands co-operated in extending the road to the marshes by making reed mats and heaping earth on to the mats to give them the appearance of a solid road.

The sentries were overpowered—there were only two—and the Russians stripped the dead Germans of their uniforms and put them on two of their number who waited for the traffic. When a convoy of tanks came along, the new sentries directed them straight into the marsh. The false road had been mined with dynamite.

The leading tank travelled a surprising distance, according to the writer, before it gradually sank beneath the reeds. Vehicles following were unaware of the trap until it was too late. Then followed a mad confusion. Dynamite explosions mingled with the tearing rat-tat of machine-gun fire and pieces of metal crashed against whole tanks as the Nazis tried to understand what was happening.

The authoress estimated that at least six tanks were

Artificial Road Leading to Marshland.

accounted for by this ambush. A fellow-guerilla believed that more had been destroyed.

This ruse is scarcely one which would succeed more than once, but its audacity sets an impressive standard.

Tanks were used for street fighting in France, but it is unlikely that they will be used elsewhere. With the defenders cashing in richly on all the chances of ambush—and in built-up areas these chances are perhaps even more numerous than in rural districts—armoured fighting vehicles stand little chance.

Open country is the nearest approach to paradise for tank men. Real open country. Not the coppice-bound localities where defenders find plenty of cover, but flat land where the few trees or shrubs living there have an endless struggle for existence in an otherwise barren waste.

Experiences in Russia show that the Nazis treat woodland with the greatest respect; tank commanders feel much safer when their charges can travel along roads which do not skirt forests.

It is true that tanks passed through Rouen in spite of the presence of anti-tank guns, but this was because the French had laid the guns to enfilade main thoroughfares while the tanks advanced in zigzag fashion down side streets. I don't mean that the tanks moved across the streets like a steamer trying to avoid a U-boat attack.

The line of advance was through side streets, then square with the anti-tank guns (being shielded from them by the tall buildings and hopping across the enfilades at irregular intervals) and forward again down another side street, and so on.

Troops were not permitted to use buildings for defence points in some areas for fear the property might be damaged!

KNOW YOUR OWN DISTRICT.

THE importance of knowing his own locality as thoroughly as he knows his own house is something which should be urged on every Home Guard. The disposition of natural defences and his ability to take maximum advantage of such conditions as road bends and indentations, dead ground, hiding holes—all these things will help him to combat the menace of invasion.

Fieldcraft and infantry training are preliminaries to successful tank-busting.

The book just mentioned deals with the experiences of one woman guerilla who had no knowledge of warfare until her locality was overrun. Many of her friends had had but slightly more. Yet in spite of their lack of training, experience and equipment, they succeeded in smashing tanks, trains, lorries, arms and general war accessories of the Nazis in addition to accounting for a considerable number of troops who would have been extra opposition for the Soviet army later.

A Stockholm message described the difficulties the Nazis met when occupying towns as they made their abortive push towards Moscow. This dispatch said that cunningly-laid mines were a nightmare to the intruders. Keys and handles turned in doors, lavatory chains pulled, taps turned on, cupboards opened—these and many others were the acts by which the evacuating Russians invited the Nazis to blow themselves to pieces.

It's no good detailing here a list of the ways you can prepare your locality for a similar welcome. Why make invasion easier by telling the enemy what to expect? But the eagerness—almost enthusiastic glee—with which Russians burned their homes, laid booby traps, destroyed crops and formed guerilla bands was an example to the rest of the world and an indication that at least one country knew how Fascist warfare should be met.

So far, invasion has not reached some countries, and in Britain the Home Guard has used this postponement to grow from a pitchfork parade to a steel-fisted heavyweight. But have local units decided where they will store their S.I.P. and thermos grenades? Have they arranged for two and possibly three alternatives?

It will be realised from the description of the S.I.P. that it is folly to leave it about for the enemy to smash with lucky shots. Both the S.I.P. and the thermos are dangerous when left in the open.

The safest place for storing the former is beneath water. They certainly must not be left in buildings likely to be affected by enemy action. The cases in which they are delivered, twenty-four at a time, and partitioned, makes it possible to lower them with safety into streams or ponds where they are least likely to do damage if exploded.

PASSIVE RESISTANCE.

Unlike the famous river, tanks cannot go on for ever.

One of the biggest arguments against their perpetual motion is the need for refuelling. One hundred miles is considered the maximum distance for any tank at one fuelling. This mileage depends, obviously, upon the country over which the vehicle is travelling and the speed at which it is being driven. The Americans claim to have raised this figure, and the Russians were experimenting at one time with a method of using again the gases from the exhaust.

The petrol tender, however, keeps up well with the vehicles and is considered to be an integral part of the attacking forces. It is the stragglers' mobile oasis, and as they advance, leapfrog fashion, their life blood is brought to them so that they can return to action.

The tender is protected much more lightly than the main cruisers and is vulnerable to attack from the air. Generally, it is kept well hidden, the petrol reaching the tanks in flat tin containers.

During the operations against Flanders and the rest of France, the Nazis found an easier way of improving their mileage. It may have been individual enterprise; it may have been part of the general instructions to Panzer divisions. Anyhow, panic-stricken garage proprietors fleeing in terror left these petrol-thirsty monsters a good store of revitalising nectar all ready for the shifting.

An important lesson emerges from this. In the event of unexpected attack, such deposits must never be allowed to fall into the hands of the invader.

"Scorched Earth" is an expression of which most people know the meaning. Petrol will help no end to put this stratagem into operation.

So, destroy petrol dumps if there is danger of their falling into enemy hands. With the absence of help from thoughtless evacuees or unresisting civilians similar to that which made his earlier advances so simple, the tank commander will have to depend on his petrol tender. Drivers of these reservoirs had a much easier job in 1940 because there was little opposition from the air.

The position is different now. The aerial opposition to the attacking Nazi forces is greater than the enemy thought could be accumulated against him—possibly because he anticipated victory much earlier.

AND *ACTIVE* RESISTANCE.

TANK-BUSTING becomes a job for everyone. The garage proprietor who destroys his petrol dump and sabotages his tools and the rural Home Guard who prepares a seductive booby trap are helping just as much as the pilot equipped with a plane built specially to resist light anti-aircraft fire and provided with armour-piercing shells fired from a light cannon.

Soviet War News reported on December 7, 1941, that one hundred and twenty-nine tanks were accounted for by one plane alone. 129!!! What a voracious appetite!

Presumably, some of this total fell to that one plane while they were harbouring. It has already been said that a stationary tank is a better target than one which is on the move. And earlier, a French communique stated that it was estimated that the German losses in five days in June included one thousand tanks. These figures give a rough impression of the size of the Nazi tank armada.

At the beginning of the war, it is likely that the charge of being unsporting would have been levelled at him who fired at a stationary target, just as the shootin' gentleman who unloaded his shotgun at a sitting bird earned the reproof of other members of the party.

Not so now. Conceptions have changed where tanks are concerned. Needs must. . . . And the present enemy has proved his devilishness abundantly.

With this in mind, the importance of harrying the invader becomes patent. He must be made to travel farther than he wanted to, and his ventilation must be so restricted, by minimising the chance of travelling with inlets and roof open and with fumes, smoke and flames to be expected at every turn, that by the end of the day's run—if ever he gets that far—the crew are completely exhausted.

The motor-cycle scouts may have found harbours for the men, or because the battle was so fluid the tank crews may have returned to one they themselves noticed during their advance. The commander, exercising caution, wants to put his unit beyond the range of the defenders. Wherever they seek to hide, they must be rooted out.

Woods, farms, or places which give good concealment from the air as well as a chance of protection against patrols will be their choice.

In spite of newspaper reports describing night tank battles in Libya, A.F.Vs. operate mostly during daylight. One Press dispatch touched an interesting note when it described eventide activity. Apparently, the experience of early American settlers has proved useful to the combatants of this war. A convoy of covered wagons attacked by Indians used to draw up in a circle, the settlers operating from behind what cover they found inside the ring.

Protection in Libya.
(The supply vehicles, etc., which would occupy the interior, have been omitted for clarity.)

This method of protection, according to the dispatch referred to, has been repeated in the Libyan desert. It is scarcely likely, however, that such tactics will be adopted elsewhere than in desert areas. Sleep in safety is a human weakness, and it is safer to hide beneath trees and barns than remain in the open, inviting the attention of night patrols. In countries where the population and rural activity is not so sparse as Libya, tanks can be expected to lie in belts of trees, coppices, farmyards, and similar protective spots.

Tank-busters operating in districts with which they are familiar must anticipate possible harbours, and where practicable, these places should be rigged so as to make them untenable. Ideas will readily suggest themselves to resourceful men. Here are two suggestions.

In a coppice where the trees are fairly close together, a tank will find difficulty in moving forward if the trees are sawn off about three feet from the ground. Usually there is not enough wood for the tank to bite into and push the stump out by the roots, yet it is too high to climb over.

Where a barn or farm building suggests itself as a possible harbour, the ground skirting it might be rendered awkward by digging ditches deep enough to contain the tracks so that the tank becomes perched on its belly. Harbouring will be only temporarily delayed, but used in conjunction with well-placed mines or traps, this scheme will add to the general nuisance tactics.

Such schemes as these should be drawn up so that when the threat of invasion becomes reality, the plans can be put into immediate execution.

Should the tank have settled in a suitable harbour, the crew must be denied rest. Doubtless the supporting infantry will form some sort of protective barrier, sentries being on duty constantly and others standing by for instant action. They will be weird soldiers if they don't.

Nuisance tactics all the time—that is the goal, if it is found impossible to attack and immobilise the invaders. But resourceful commanders will see ways of penetrating to the vehicles.

A preliminary reconnaissance will give information on which a night attack against harbouring vehicles should be planned. The commander decides how the attack is to be conducted, remembering that the tank itself will be turned into a gun emplacement if the crew can reach it before the attackers have cashed in on their advantage of surprise.

WRECKING.

As tanks achieve most by striking suddenly, so do tank smashers. A stealthy, unheralded approach, followed immediately by smashing blows, is the objective.

One important point to be remembered is that if the vehicles are at all likely to be recaptured by the enemy, they must be made absolutely useless. Their repair shops and recovery organisation have already acquired a high reputation. Minor battles, apparently out of all proportion to the prize, have been waged by the Nazis simply to recover one immobilised vehicle.

Therefore, those tanks which cannot be sent back for examination by experts and possible use by our forces to places well beyond the reach of the invader must be dealt with in such a way that even if the enemy does get them again, they will be more trouble than they are worth.

Smashing the tracks is not good enough. Since these are constantly needing repair, the mechanics are already efficient to a high degree in replacing them. The workshop may even carry whole tracks. A high explosive bomb does the job of wrecking pretty well, if it is a rush job.

Sledge hammers directed at the water jacket, carburetter (in those models where carburetters are fixed—the majority have a fuel pump system), and driver's controls and other fitments inside will spoil the usefulness of a tank.

No sledge hammer? If you've any initiative, you'll find something to do so much damage that your prey will never run again. How about leaving one or two S.I.Ps. inside and lobbing another through the lid?

STICKY BOMBS.

A COUPLE of sticky bombs, one on top of the other, should rip a hole somewhere. Decide first where you will take cover before the fuses have burnt out, or you won't be allowed to review your handiwork.

Sticky bombs. They've had quite a lot of publicity, and you'd like to know something about them. Obviously, a full description is impossible.

The bomb is shaped like an oversized orange and is held by a thick, stick-like handle which is screwed into the main portion and carries a detonator inserted immediately before the bomb is to be used. An outer casing of metal falls away with the removal of a pin, and the sticky sphere is disclosed. Don't handle this surface. If you do, your fingers will get in such a mess that bomb-throwing will be an impossibility. You might even be tempted to release your grip on the detonating handle.

Unless the grenade is held so that the casing falls clear as the casing cover pin is removed, this shell is likely to get stuck to the tacky surface. Having prepared the "sticky," a safety pin is next removed, and until the detonating handle is released, nothing will happen.

Throwing or dropping this bomb from a slit trench or a height are recommended as two methods of disposing of it, but the most effective way, in the case of stationary tanks, is to plant it on a vulnerable point—firmly, so as to break the glass h.e. container—and duck under cover.

During an offensive against A.F.Vs., it is necessary to put the crews out of action. If there is a S.I.P. dripping fire and belching fumes around the louvre, the crew may surrender. Should they decide to stay inside their vehicle, they must be dug out. As long as they are inside, their guns are a menace. A sticky bomb (the official name is "S.T. grenade") planted on the lid will shake them up. The skull of a tank is always more lightly armoured than the body.

They're still holding out? Point-blank rifle fire through the slits ought to make them change their minds, and grenades exploding under the belly or a hand grenade, such as the h.e. 36, lobbed through a rip in the plating, will do the trick.

The Soviet Information Bureau thought enough of the efforts of one Red soldier, in urging a crew to leave their shelter, to give him a special mention in a communique. His method was to jump on a tank and slam with a sledge hammer until the men inside could stand it no longer. Apparently the Germans found the din insufferable, and, being unable to tell what was going on outside, they had to open up. Riflemen standing by finished off those who did not surrender.

S.T. grenades may be detonated by attaching a length of string to the safety pin, which the operator tugs out after he has taken cover. The pin, in this case, must be adjusted so that it will slip out easily. Then the grenadier plants his bomb on a vulnerable spot and detonates it from a safe distance.

LATER INVENTIONS STILL.

Mr. Churchill has made reference to another device: the Bombard. Apart from saying that this has a most "depressing" effect on A.F.Vs., nothing more can be mentioned.

Other weapons have appeared and continue to appear. A new type of percussion grenade has been introduced and a completely modern design of anti-tank gun has been referred to enthusiastically by Lord Beaverbrook in the House of Lords. Is it conceivable that tanks will become so vulnerable as to lose their value in warfare?

Flame-throwing devices are part of the equipment of the Regular Army. Attention to wind directions and strength of the jet will determine when and how these devices will be used. A news reel containing shots of the Turkish Army during manœuvres showed a soldier using flame-throwing apparatus. He crawled along, gripping the nozzle which was connected to a container, and directed a jet of flame at an imaginary objective. In this film it was noticed that he could turn on the jet at will and the liquid ignited almost immediately.

The British Army has been training with flame-throwers and has paid attention to the potentialities of fire as a servant at all times, and since the Dunkirk evacuation has increased its interest in this sphere of warfare.

As a means of conducting warfare, fire has a long history.

Dropping boiling oil on warriors who were in the act of assaulting a fort is often mentioned by ancient writers as being a favourite trick of those defending the stronghold.

Shooting flaming arrows at the covered wagons referred to on page 40 was an aggravating habit of Red Indians.

In the last war, our airmen's use of flaming darts against zeppelins was mistakenly described as being the Germans using liquid fire.

Suicide squads who crept towards enemy trenches with containers full of inflammable liquid strapped to their backs often succeeded in dislodging gunners from machine-gun nests or burning troops out of a strong point—at least, for a time.

Security reasons will not permit a description of the various flame-throwing devices which the Nazis will meet, but it can be said with confidence that they are in for a hot time.

TANKS IN TOWNS.

THE earlier description of a tank advance being made with motor-cycle scouts forming the advance guard is not necessarily true when the column is descending upon a village or town. Indeed, these lightly protected troops have learnt that when approaching built-up places they must seek the protection of the tanks which in such conditions are now moving up cautiously.

Road blocks will have been arranged in order to make their approach less of a roving commission than it was in the early stages of this war. Concrete blocks and tank ditches will have been arranged so that their movements are confined to roads where at strategic points gunners in block-houses can immobilise them.

These obstacles are the traffic regulators which even tanks must obey. With such directors, anti-tank squads will have a chance of waiting in ambush, knowing that the tanks must pass across their front.

In the first Russo-Finnish campaign, a Finn was commended for jumping on to an approaching tank from his cover, opening the lid and dropping a hand grenade inside. That is the sort of argument which will convince Nazi tank-drivers that they are expected to stop.

It might be thought that an attacker adopting such tactics would have no chance of surviving the fire of following tanks, but experience has shown that it is difficult to get a perfect aim at such short range at a man target moving rapidly from cover. Just as tanks benefit by speed, so the tank-buster makes speed of movement his ally. That is why Spaniards found it possible to smash the tracks with crowbars and bits of iron.

Men training in anti-tank warfare must learn *when* to move from cover. You might at first think that the movement of mice who have been surprised in your kitchen have nothing to do with this, but they can teach you valuable lessons. (Provided, of course, you suffer from mice!)

Watch them, next time you suddenly switch on the light and hear their scufflings. They dive for cover immediately, and remain there perfectly still until the position is endangered; then, another bound and they are gone before offensive action can be taken against them.

Similarly with tank-hunters. They must wait until the guns are directed away from them, then dart to a spot where the guns, when they are swivelled round, will have no effect. Meanwhile, other tank-busters will take advantage of their being not covered and will make a hop nearer to their objective. That is where the analogy between mice and tank-busters ceases. The rodents are seeking their own protection; the troops are making the tank crews feel mouse-like, and are on the offensive.

Summarised, the lesson to be learned is that when men are detailed for tank smashing, they must move separately, speedily, in short bounds, and when the guns are not pointed in their direction.

There is just as much cover in town districts as in rural areas. If bombers and heavy artillery have been active, the chances for concealment are probably greater. The tactics to be employed in towns, just as in the country, are woven around the local conditions, emphasis being laid at all times on two essentials: speed and surprise.

Burn, blast, blind, bust. Decoy, destroy, and then drag out the crew.

When those things have been done, the Nazis who have sought to smash their way through the opposition with metallic superiority must be put out of action, and if the tank is not wanted for examination, it must be rendered useless.

AMERICAN TANK-CHASER.

A DESCRIPTION of an American tank-chaser appeared in the Press in December, 1941, and the possibilities of such a vehicle being successful appear good.

Characteristics: high road speed, combined with mobility over rough and soft terrain. Powered with a 147-h.p. engine, it weighs 8¾ tons and carries armour and half-track. There is a two-way radio, two machine-guns of .30 calibre, another of .50 calibre, and its 75-mm. gun is capable of stopping any armoured vehicle it meets. It will travel at 50 miles an hour when necessary and can cruise two hundred and fifty miles before the petrol tank needs to be refilled.

This machine has the advantage over static defence. The tank-fighter on foot has to wait for his quarry and strike when the opportunity presents itself, but the tank chaser is the land E-boat which can run faster than its prey.

The military expression of offensive defence is typified in this latest war weapon.

HOW TANKS STARTED.

THE British were responsible for originating tank warfare, the first model making its appearance on the Somme in September, 1916.

Mr. Winston Churchill was one of the few proponents of the novelty, which met with opposition from British G.H.Q., and from generals on both sides of the English Channel. Indeed, Lord Kitchener himself twice rejected the scheme.

Engineers had submitted many designs to the War Office between 1911 and 1914. One, found in the depths of a War Office pigeon-hole, bore the brief and almost decisive—certainly derisive—comment: "The man's mad." Such was the official attitude.

Fifteen tanks eventually arrived in France in August, 1916, and went into action for the first time on September 15, being withdrawn in November because the mudfield which was the battlefield held them immobile.

Towards the end of that war, however, they reappeared, and in July, 1918, there were 34 Tank Corps battalions, each with 72 tanks.

The earliest models had two large cartwheels at the rear, and the armament was fitted into sponsons or casemates, one on each side. The traverse of their guns seems to have been greater than in modern types, but because of this the machines were more vulnerable. There was no protection for the caterpillar tracks, and a large exhaust pipe trailed over the roof to the rear. On the roof was a wire netting bomb protector, which may have succeeded then but which certainly would be ineffective now. The speed of these vehicles seldom exceeded walking pace.

Wire netting over armoured cars and vehicles was often used as protection against bombs, and this gave birth to what was probably the first sticky bomb—of a type. It made its appearance in Ireland, at the time of the Sinn Fein disturbances, and consisted of an ordinary bomb, with the additional fitment of hooks. The "thrower" had to see that the hooks engaged in the netting, and usually they were placed in position in the same way as is advocated with its modern offspring.

The need for speed was responsible for the introduction of whippet tanks, named after the fleet-footed dogs. These were capable of twice the speed of their forerunners, and appeared on the Western Front as the war came to a close. They were of greater use for reconnaissance, raiding and pursuit.

In 1918, the German High Command, admitting defeat, reported: "Two factors have been decisive: first the tanks . . ."

It will be a fitting conclusion to this war when the German High Command finds itself having to report: "Two factors have been decisive: first the tank-fighters . . ."

ANTI-TANK WEAPONS
Smash The Tank

An insight into the amateur side of World War 2. Diagrams illustrate the main points and the devices, such as the Thermos Bomb;Phosrhorus Bomb;Sticky Bombs; that could be cobbled together from household items are described.This pamphlet was available to the Home Guard and describes the German tank and how to destroy it. It is an early War publication c1940, dealing with the light tanks used by the Germans, also the author gives examples of anti-tank actions in the Spanish Civil War, in which he took part. I'ts is a fascinating look at the "enthusiastic" approach to killing tanks.

9781474539449

TANK HUNTING AND DESTRUCTION 1940

The stated object for the distributing of this War Office manual was as "A guide and help to troops who have the determination and nerve to destroy tanks at close quarters". Intended for fighting on home soil after the very real possibility of a full German invasion, "Operation Sea Lion", this is a remarkable if somewhat naive snap shot of Britain state of preparedness,in her most dangerous hour.

The contents details Tank hunting, Tank characteristics,Tactical action,Road blocks,ambushes Ect,also includes an interesting appendix on Molotov Cocktails, and materials on other ways to destroy tanks.

9781474539401

TROOP TRAINING FOR LIGHT TANK TROOPS NOVEMBER 1939

Very early War tactics pertaining to various aspects of training with and employing armour in the British Army. Covering in concise detail that which a Light tank crew needed to know to be effective in action. In the early years of the war, Germany held the initiative. German forces used Blitzkrieg tactics in France in 1940, making full use of the speed and armour of tanks to break through enemy defences. It was clear that German tank tactics had evolved during the inter-war period. By contrast, Britain and the Allies were playing catch-up.

9781474539302

JAPANESE WEAPONS ILLUSTRATED
September 1944

This period 'Restricted' laced binding manual was intended to be an aid to the identification of Japanese Army equipment, with sections covering: Tanks, both two-man, Tankette, light and medium; Armoured Cars; Self-Propelled Guns; Anti-Tank Guns; Artillery; Anti-Aircraft Guns; Mortars & Grenade Dischargers; Small Arms; Flamethrowers etc. Produced one year before the surrender of Japan, this work gives a good overview of the weapons the allies would find, fighting an army that despite being on the back foot, was still capable of stiff resistance in an almost entirely defensive role..

9781474539432

NOTES ON THE GERMAN ARMY-WAR
December 1940

An early war 393-page 'Notes' periodical manual from December 1940. It is a detailed review, for use in the field. The manual looks at every aspect of the "Blitzkrieg" German Army (and, to some extent, the Air Force) and gives details as known at the time.

It covers the fighting arms and the services behind them – tactics, organisation, weapons and equipment. It usefully also includes a colour section on uniforms and insignia, a black-and-white plate section of small arms, infantry support and anti-tank weapons, artillery and AFVs. A series of pull-outs related to the text covering tanks etc. are also reproduced.

This is an important first-class picture of the complex fighting machine that was the German Army at the end of the campaigns of 1940, only six months before the invasion of Russia.

9781474539203

GERMAN MINES AND TRAPS

Mid-1940 War Office manual with details of German mines, both the Teller and S-mine (Bouncing Betty) are covered, with techniques for disarming. Good clear full-page line drawings give both practical and technical information. Highly recommended because of the illustrations, which show how these devices worked and the components.

9781474535809

NOTES ON ENEMY ARMY IDENTIFICATIONS ITALY
October 1941

This period handbook was published to give British military personnel a better understanding of the principal characteristics of both the Italian army and the Black Shirt Militia under active service conditions , it is dated October 1941.

It begins with a description of distinctive branches, or specialities, the most characteristic of which was the arm of the Royal Carabinieri, a semi-military body occupying, historically, the senior position in the Army. Other specialities included the Grenadiers of Sardinia, the Bersaglieri, the Alpini and the San Marco Marine Regiment

The handbook then goes on to show, in order, the organisation of Command and Staff, of formations (corps and divisions) and of the arms and services; services, supply and transportation; ranks, plates (many in colour) cover uniforms, insignia, medals and decorations; armament and equipment and a chapter on the Air Force, There are chapters on tactical doctrine and principles of employment, on permanent fortifications, camouflage and abbreviations. Finally there is a brief index.

9781474539746

MANUAL OF GUERILLA TACTICS
Specially Prepared And Based On Lessons From The Spanish And Russian Campaigns

One of the excellent, concise Bernards Pocket Books, intended to show members of the Home Guard and the regular forces that war is not conducted in a gentlemanly way – it is kill or be killed.

9781474539463

THE OFFENSIVE OF SMALL UNITS
September 1916

This is a periodical tactical manual from 1916, it focuses on the manner in which the French organised and executed their attacks and counterattacks . Summarised from the French, it lays out the process by which to operate in attacks on the German trenches. Focused purely on the operation of infantry, the purpose of this British translation is to give small infantry units the benefit of the French experience in regard to the best methods of combat, in offensive operations.

9781474537971

TRENCH WARFARE
Notes on attack and defence, February 1915

This important period manual was published in early 1915 when hope of a quick ending to the war disappeared, and trench warfare had begun to dominate the Western Front.

The manual strives to instil an offensive spirit and gives practical examples on: Close quarter, local, methods of successful warfare, and German attacks. The salient points to gather were preparation and co-operation between artillery and infantry, and that the capture of trenches is easier than their retention. Two plates illustrating tactics complete this official publication.

9781474539807

Ministry Of Home Security
OBJECTS DROPPED FROM THE AIR 1941

An illustrated Official and confidential publication, covering the many and varied types of objects that were falling from principally German aircraft during the Second phase of the blitz, including high explosives,incendiary bombs and small arms ammunition. Complete with 8 page addendum.

9781783319541

THE MUSKETRY INSTRUCTIONS
FOR THE GERMAN INFANTRY 1887
(Schiessvorshrift fur die Infanterie)
Translated for the intelligence Division War Office

Translated for the War Office by Colonel C W Bowdler Bell

A facsimile that includes the supplement for the German Infantry for 1887. Musketry exercises were intended to give the infantry instruction in shooting, to make effective use of their firearm in battle. As such the manual shows important details designed to make the infantry soldier battle-ready by the end of his first year of service. Instruction is subdivided into Preparatory exercises; Target practice; Field firing; Instructional firing; Inspection in musketry; Proving the rifle M/61.84 and revolver M/83. Many black powder weapons were still used, mainly for training purposes, up to end of the First World War.

9781783313631

www.ingramcontent.com/pod-product-compliance
Lightning Source LLC
Chambersburg PA
CBHW071645040426
42452CB00009B/1769
* 9 7 8 1 4 7 4 5 3 9 4 4 9 *